© 2020 by Raj Haldar and Chris Carpenter • Cover and internal illustrations by Bryce Gladfelter • Cover and internal design © 2020 by Sourcebooks
The Worst Ever and *P Is for Pterodactyl* are trademarks of Raj Haldar.

The full color art was hand-drawn with ink, then layered with digital color.

Published by Sourcebooks eXplore, an imprint of Sourcebooks Kids • P.O. Box 4410, Naperville, Illinois 60567-4410 • (630) 961-3900 • sourcebookskids.com

Library of Congress Cataloging-in-Publication Data is on file with the publisher.

Source of Production: 1010 Printing Asia Limited, North Point, Hong Kong, China • Date of Production: September 2020 • Run Number: 5019913 • Printed and bound in China. • OGP 10 9 8 7 6 5 4 3

You can't believe everything you hear! Did you know that a single word can have many different meanings, and sometimes words that sound alike can be spelled completely differently? In this book, Ptolemy predicts you'll find that two sentences may sound exactly the same, but they can mean hilariously different things!

NO READING ALLOWED*

*THE WORST READ-ALOUD BOOK EVER**

**A confusing collection of hilarious homonyms and sound-alike sentences.

FROM THE #1 *NEW YORK TIMES* BESTSELLING
CREATORS OF *P IS FOR PTERODACTYL*
RAJ HALDAR & CHRIS CARPENTER

PICTURES BY
BRYCE GLADFELTER

SOURCEBOOKS eXplore

The hair came forth.

The hare came fourth.

We were all astonished by the fowl feat.

We were all astonished by the foul feet.

The mummy prepared farro for dinner.

The mummy prepared pharaoh for dinner.

They mustered everything but couldn't catch up. We relished it.

They mustard everything but couldn't ketchup. We relished it.

They bowled in all caps.

"They" (bold, in all caps)

She had all the dough she could knead.

She had all the dough she could need.

It's raining cats and dogs.

It's reigning cats and dogs.

The pool queue is far too long.

The pool cue is far too long.

His pants are tapered.

His pants are tapired.

The new deli clerk runs a pretty sorry store.

The New Delhi clerk runs a pretty sari store.

Sir Francis Bacon

Sir, France is bakin'!

Orion's Belt is out.

Oh, Ryan's belt is out!

My Navy father had blue jeans. My mother was well-read.
They marooned me.

My navy father had blue genes. My mother was, well, red.
They marooned me.

The barred man looted the establishment.

The bard man luted the establishment.

The hero had super vision.

The hero had supervision.

Hear their herd?

Here, they're heard!

The fearsome predator preys.

The "fearsome predator" prays.

The barn is raised.

The barn is razed.

Stu...? Where's Stu when it's time to eat?

Stu wears stew when it's time to eat.

We see the queen's burrow thanks to our ant hill.

We see the Queensboro thanks to our Aunt Hill.

The children scarfed the mousse.

The children scarfed the moose.

Beware the sharp turn.

Beware the sharp tern.

The pitcher held the batter.

The pitcher held the batter.

Man, a tea sounds great.

Manatee sounds great!

The fryer sizzled on the range.

The friar sizzled on the range.

C Major...it's a beautiful key.

See, Major? It's a beautiful quay.

The miners rode with ores.

The minors rowed with oars.

Four mermaids jump over the good gnus.

Former maids jump over the good news.

It's fun to read this book if it isn't aloud.

It's fun to read this book if it isn't allowed.

The Worst Glossary Ever...Again!

allow (v.)—To permit something to happen.

aloud (adv.)—When something is said or a noise is made in a way that it can be easily heard.

bard (n.)—An old-fashioned name for a person who composes and recites long poems, usually while playing a harp or some other stringed instrument. The poet and playwright William Shakespeare is often called "The Bard of Avon," because he's from a village in England called Stratford-upon-Avon.

barred (adj.)—When something is covered by a set of bars, such as a person who has been sent to jail.

bold (adj.)—When words are printed with thick, dark print so that they're easily seen or emphasized.

bowl (v.)—To roll a ball towards something, especially in the oh-so-fun game of bowling, where players roll a heavy ball down a wooden lane aiming to knock down as many white pins as possible. Knock down all ten and it's a strike!

caps
1. (n.)—Coverings that are worn on people's heads; any kind of hat.
2. (adj.)—A shorthand way of saying "capitalized." We use the phrase "all caps" when something is written in all capital letters.

cue (n.)—A long, thin stick that is used by players of pool, billiards, and snooker to hit balls across the (usually) green felt table. The earliest documented record of a billiard table was made in 1470 in an inventory of the possessions of King Louis XI of France! (*see* queue)

fearsome (adj.)—When a person or thing appears to be very scary and frightening; causing fear.

farro (n.)—A type of grain, similar to rice, that was commonly eaten in ancient times and has become popular again as a healthy food. (*see* pharaoh)

forth (adv.)—When something comes onward or outward; out into notice or view. (*see* fourth)

foul (adj.)—Very unpleasant taste or smell. Yuck! (*see* fowl)

fourth (adv.)—Coming next after third in a series. (*see* forth)

fowl (n.)—The general term for a barnyard bird, like a chicken, hen, or rooster. (*see* foul)

friar (n.)—A male member of a religious group known for wearing long woolen robes and spreading the teachings of Christianity. In the Middle Ages (and all the way up until 1972), friars shaved the tops of their heads in a perfect circle—a very distinctive hair style called a tonsure.

fryer (n.)—A kitchen implement for frying foods.

gnu (n.)—Also known by the fun-to-say name "wildebeest," these stocky, ox-like antelopes can be spotted by their distinct curved horns as they graze on the African plains. (*see* news)

hair (n.)—A thin, thread-like growth from the skin of a person or animal; the stuff that grows on your head. Did you know that the world's longest human hair is over eighteen feet? That's about as long as a giraffe is tall!

hare (n.)—A rodent-like mammal in the rabbit family that is known for being fast on its feet. Hares can run up to speeds of forty-five mph.

hear (v.)—To be aware of sound through your ears. Did you know that dogs can hear much higher-pitched sounds than humans can?

here (adv.)—At this location; in this place.

heard (v.)—To have learned or perceived by the ear.

herd (n.)—A group of animals that live or are kept together.

key (n.)—The musical scale around which a song revolves. (*see* quay)

knead (v.)—To mix something, usually dough, by pressing it with your hands. Bread is one of the oldest foods eaten by humans and can be made with a dough consisting of flour and water. (*see* need)

loot (v.)—To steal something; to plunder.

lute (n.)—A stringed instrument like a pear-shaped guitar with a rounded back.

manatee (n.)—A large, plant-eating, aquatic mammal with two flippers in the front and a broad, spoon-shaped tail. It's thought that these cow-like creatures of the sea might have inspired early mermaid tales!

maroon
1. (adj.)—A dark red color.
2. (v.)—To leave on a deserted island; the preferred punishment of pirates.

miner (n.)—A person who works in a mine to unearth things like metals or precious stones, like diamonds. Gold and copper were among the first metals discovered by ancient people.

minor (n.)—Someone too young to have the same rights as an adult; another word for a kid like you.

mustard (n.)—A yellow or brownish sauce made from the mustard plant. It goes perfectly with hot dogs! Mustard may have been one of the first condiments used by humans. Dig it! Egyptian pharaohs stocked their tombs with mustard seeds to take into the afterlife.

muster (v.)—To work hard to find or get something; to gather.

need (v.)—To have to have something; to require. (*see* knead)

news (n.)—Information that is reported in a newspaper, magazine, or internet website. In ancient Rome, around 59 BC, early forms of newspapers were etched into stone or metal and displayed in public places. (*see* gnu)

New Delhi (n.)—The capital city of India. Did you know the city of New Delhi has the largest spice market *and* the largest vegetable market in all of Asia?

oar (n.)—A large pole that is flat on one end; used to row and steer a boat. Wooden oars dating back to 5,000 BC have been discovered in China.

ore (n.)—A piece of rock or earth that contains precious metals.

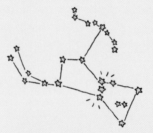

Orion's Belt (n.)—Part of the constellation Orion, which is named after a hunter in Greek mythology; the three bright stars that form the hunter's sword belt. Orion is one of the most recognizable and easiest-to-find constellations in the night sky!

pharaoh (n.)—A ruler in ancient Egypt. Pharaohs are famous for building pyramids as their own tombs. Up until the completion of the Lincoln Cathedral in 1311, the Great Pyramid of Giza was considered the tallest man-made structure for more than 3,800 years. (*see* farro)

pray (v.)—To wish very much for something to happen.

prey (v.)—To hunt something; usually when a big animal hunts a smaller one.

quay (n.)—The place where ships load and unload passengers. You might remember this word from our first book, *P Is for Pterodactyl*! (*see* key)

Queensboro (n.)—Also known as Queensborough or just Queens. One of the five boroughs that make up New York City, the awesome borough of Queens is one of the most diverse places in the United States, with residents from every corner of the world. Queens was also chosen as the site of the 1964 World's Fair.

queue (n.)—A line of people waiting for something. (*see* cue)

rain (v.)—When water falls to the Earth in droplets. Time to play in the puddles! (*see* reign)

raise (v.)—To lift or move something. In farming communities, it's when the whole community gets together to help one farmer construct a new barn.

raze (v.)—To completely destroy or dismantle something; usually a building (or your pillow fort!).

reign (n.)—The period of time during which a king or queen rules a country; or as long as you hold any record, say, for fastest shower in your family! (*see* rain)

relish
1. (v.)—To enjoy or take pleasure in something.
2. (n.)—A condiment made of chopped fruits and vegetables that's used to add flavor to any food (particularly hot dogs!).

sari (n.)—A garment of clothing traditionally worn by women and girls in India, where one long and beautiful piece of cloth is wrapped around the body and shoulders.

Sir Francis Bacon (n.)—An English philosopher and author who has been described as one of the greatest thinkers ever. Sir Francis Bacon is often called the father of the scientific method, making experimentation the most important part of scientific discovery.

supervision (n.)—The action of directing what someone does or how something is done.

tapered (adj.)—When the shape of something becomes smaller towards one end; like your stylish new jeans!

tapir (n.)—A pig-like animal with a long nose and short legs that can be found in the tropical parts of America and Asia. A typical tapir can weigh somewhere between five hundred and eight hundred pounds.

tern (n.)—A type of bird that usually lives near the ocean. Most terns have long wings, forked tails, and sharply pointed beaks. Grab those bird-hunting binoculars and remember to take *turns!*

turn (n.)—The place at which a road or trail changes direction.

wear (v.)—To use or put something on as clothing.

where (adv.)—In what place.

We're the worst!*

*You may have noticed a handful of words in this book that have been used in unusual ways for the sake of humor.

For example, the words mustard and relish aren't usually used as verbs when it comes to adding yummy condiments to your hot dog. We even created a new way to use the word "marooned" (not in the sense of a castaway, but "to turn something the color maroon"). Last but not least, this book is probably the first and only time you'll ever see the made-up word, "tapired" where our jungle explorer has a few furry tapirs taped to his trousers!

We're just having some fun here, but the truth is that our language is always changing. Did you know that hundreds of new words are added to the dictionary each year? Maybe a word that you made up will be next!